Books so fun you'll pee your pants!™

Truth or Dare!™

kids

made you laugh!™

Editorial Director: Erin Conley
Designers: Hallie Warshaw and Tanya Napier/Orange Avenue™
Special thanks to Suzanne Cracraft, Maria Llull, Jeanette Miller and Nancy
Spector for their invaluable assistance!

ISBN 1-57528-927-X

TABLE OF CONTENTS

TRUTH OR DARE

3

INTRODUCTION

Who knows what I'd be doing now if I hadn't spent so much of my childhood playing games? Board games, card games, party games ... I relished them all. Truth or Dare taught me when to take a risk and when to play it safe. It also taught me a lot about my friends and myself. Games like Truth or Dare made me realize that you can learn something and still have a good time. This realization inspired me to make fun and games my day job—and a way of life.

No matter how young or old, busy or stressed you are, *Truth or Dare!* is bound to bring out the kid in you!

Enjoy!
Bob

INSTRUCTIONS

OBJECT
The aim of the game is to tell the truth, take some chances and have some fun with your friends while collecting points.

PLAYING THE GAME
First things first: grab a pen and paper to keep track of your points.
- The oldest and wisest player goes first. This player picks **Truth, Dare** or **Do You Know** and THEN reads his/her challenge (from number one, page six) aloud to the group.
- *If a player accepts a* Truth or Dare! *challenge*, the group decides whether s/he has completed the challenge and whether s/he earns a point – or not!

TRUTH =1 point
DARE = 2 points
DO YOU KNOW = 1 bonus pass

- *If a player decides to skip a* Truth or Dare! *challenge*, s/he loses a point – unless a bonus pass is traded in. There's no penalty if a player has 0 points and chooses to skip a challenge. Bonus passes held until the end of the game do not count toward final score.

- Play proceeds counter-clockwise. Player Two must now choose **Truth, Dare** or **Do You Know** to see if s/he is up to the next challenge (number two, page six)!

WINNING THE GAME
The first player to collect 15 points wins the game.

TRUTH OR DARE

1 TRUTH You've just won one million dollars! How much do you give to charity?

DARE Bark a Christmas carol.

DO YOU KNOW . . . which player can tell you what kind of currency you need to buy sushi in Japan?

2 TRUTH If you could have one item of clothing from each player, what would it be?

DARE It's your very first recital. Give the tap-dancing performance of your life.

DO YOU KNOW . . . which player eats the broccoli stems?

3   **TRUTH**   You are a famous rock star with a list of items that each concert venue must provide in your dressing room. What are the first three things on your list?

       DARE   Imitate the animal you hope to be in your next life.

       DO YOU KNOW ... which player would eat something s/he dropped on the floor?

4   **TRUTH**   What would you do if you saw someone cheating on a test you were taking?

       DARE   Burp the vowels.

       DO YOU KNOW ... how the player to your left likes his/her eggs: scrambled, poached, fried or hard-boiled?

TRUTH OR DARE

7

TRUTH A friend borrowed five bucks from you last week and still hasn't paid you back. Do you mention it to him/her?

DARE Sing the lowest note you can.

DO YOU KNOW . . . which player would make the best lifeguard?

TRUTH Your teacher tells a dumb joke. Do you laugh?

DARE Show everyone in the room how good you are at breakdancing.

DO YOU KNOW . . . which player goes the longest without changing his/her socks?

7

TRUTH   If you could be any superhero, which one would you be?

DARE   Sniff the player to your left's bare foot.

DO YOU KNOW . . . which player spends the most time looking in the mirror?

8

TRUTH   Have you ever spied on someone? Who? Why?

DARE   Pretend that you're in bed having a nightmare.

DO YOU KNOW . . . which player is addicted to the Internet?

TRUTH OR DARE

TRUTH How old do you wish you were right now?

DARE Name a famous person who looks like each player in your group.

DO YOU KNOW . . . what brand of toothpaste the player to your right usually uses?

TRUTH You are in a jellybean store, surrounded by jars of loose jellybeans—do you sample before you buy?

DARE Make the player to your left laugh any way you can within 30 seconds.

DO YOU KNOW . . . which player is the biggest slacker?

TRUTH Describe what you looked like as a baby.

DARE You can't continue this relationship. Turn to the player on your right and break up with him/her.

DO YOU KNOW . . . the street address of the player to your right?

TRUTH Which player would most likely let your biggest secret slip?

DARE Confess your most ticklish spot and let the player to your left tickle you.

DO YOU KNOW . . . what day of the week the person to your right was born?

TRUTH OR DARE

TRUTH What teen idol would you most like to date?

DARE Come up with a pet "love" name (i.e. Muffin, Snookums) for each person in the room.

DO YOU KNOW ... what year the person to your right was born?

TRUTH Which player tells the worst jokes?

DARE Pick up three nearby objects and try to juggle them.

DO YOU KNOW ... which player prefers a bath to a shower?

15 **TRUTH** Tell which player is most likely to offer his/her seat on the bus to an elderly person.

DARE Yodel until the other players tell you to stop.

DO YOU KNOW ... which player owns the most shoes?

16 **TRUTH** If you could change your name, what would you change it to?

DARE Try to touch your nose with your tongue.

DO YOU KNOW ... which players have your phone number memorized? (Make them prove it!)

TRUTH OR DARE

TRUTH Ever get caught lying? Give details.

DARE Draw a face on your stomach and make it say something to the player on your left.

DO YOU KNOW . . . which player likes olives?

TRUTH A cat darts into the road. You feel a thud under your bicycle tire. Do you stop?

DARE Give us your best snort!

DO YOU KNOW . . . what was the last book the player to your left read?

19

TRUTH A classmate has bad breath. Do you say something? If so, what?

DARE You're the table. Have a conversation with the chair.

DO YOU KNOW ... what type of food the player to your left eats most often?

20

TRUTH What kind of fruit best describes the player to your right, and why?

DARE Using your lips, pick up a pen off the floor.

DO YOU KNOW ... when the player on your right last rode a bike?

TRUTH OR DARE

21 **TRUTH** What would you do if your best friend's crush flirted with you?

DARE Have an argument with yourself about what to have for dinner.

DO YOU KNOW . . . which player has been sent to the principal's office?

22 **TRUTH** If you had to move to another country for a year, which one would you choose, and why?

DARE You just won your first MTV Music Video Award®. Give your acceptance speech.

DO YOU KNOW . . . which player has been paid to baby-sit?

23

TRUTH If you could have invented something in history, including very recent history, what would it be? Why?

DARE You're a fashion critic at the Academy Awards® and the other players are movie stars. Critique their outfits.

DO YOU KNOW . . . which player can roll his/her tongue?

24

TRUTH If you only had 15 minutes left to live, what would you do?

DARE You're auditioning for the lead in a movie about the player to your right. Try to be as convincing as you can. You want this part!

DO YOU KNOW . . . all of the other players' ages?

TRUTH OR DARE

17

25 **TRUTH**   What's your least favorite color?

DARE   You're a superhero based on whatever object the player to your left hands you (i.e. "Pencil Man"/"Napkin Woman"). Get in character and tell us about your powers.

DO YOU KNOW . . . which players would eat pizza that's been sitting out overnight for breakfast?

26 **TRUTH**   If your best friend and your pet were drowning, which one would you save?

DARE   Do a rain dance.

DO YOU KNOW . . . which player has sung karaoke most recently?

27

TRUTH   What's your biggest fear?

DARE   Your head isn't screwed on right. Hold it in place for the next two minutes.

DO YOU KNOW . . . which player is the biggest junk-food junkie?

28

TRUTH   Have you ever picked something out of your teeth and eaten it?

DARE   Trade socks and shoes with the person to your left within 60 seconds. Go!

DO YOU KNOW . . . which player is a teacher's pet?

TRUTH or DARE

TRUTH Have you ever wanted to toilet-paper someone's house? Whose? Why?

DARE Take off your shoes and socks and kiss both of your feet.

DO YOU KNOW ... which player has a secret crush on a celebrity?

TRUTH What's the meanest thing you've done to a friend?

DARE Drop a piece of food on the floor, then pick it up and eat it.

DO YOU KNOW ... which player has cheated on a test?

TRUTH What smell do you dislike most? Be specific.

DARE Pretend you are a chicken and cluck "Happy Birthday."

DO YOU KNOW ... which player has the smallest feet?

TRUTH What is your worst habit?

DARE Pick all the lint out of your belly button and show it to everyone in the room.

DO YOU KNOW ... which player has been to the dentist most recently?

TRUTH OR DARE

33 **TRUTH** If you had one-million dollars to spend in only ONE store, what store would you choose?

DARE There's a new dance craze called the Whiz Burger sweeping the nation. Show us how it goes.

DO YOU KNOW . . . which player kisses his/her pet?

34 **TRUTH** If you could take only one player on a trip around the world, who would it be, and why?

DARE Call a friend and act like you think it's his/her birthday. Be sure to sing!

DO YOU KNOW . . . which player sleeps with his/her pet?

35 **TRUTH** Have you ever borrowed somebody else's underwear and worn it?

DARE Identify one thing the player to your left has that you want, and beg him/her for it.

DO YOU KNOW . . . which player is wearing dirty socks?

36 **TRUTH** If you could be a fly on a wall for a day, whose wall would you like to hang out on?

DARE You're Kermit the Frog. Tell us why it ain't easy being green.

DO YOU KNOW . . . how many players are wearing colored underwear?

TRUTH OR DARE

23

37 **TRUTH** Have you ever peed in a swimming pool?

DARE Pretend to lay a golden egg.

DO YOU KNOW . . . which players are left-handed?

38 **TRUTH** If you could trade families with someone in the room, who would it be?

DARE Without speaking, tell the story of your life while doing the hula.

DO YOU KNOW . . . which players have had chicken pox?

39

TRUTH Which player is most likely to be a star?

DARE Do your best impersonation of a blowfish and swim around the room three times.

DO YOU KNOW ... how many players have a parent born between 1959 and 1979?

40

TRUTH Name the movie star you think you most resemble.

DARE Run across the room holding a book between your legs.

DO YOU KNOW ... the favorite candy bar of the player to your left?

TRUTH OR DARE

TRUTH Which player's mind would you most like to read right now?

DARE You are trying out for a stunt double role. Show the group your most realistic trip and fall.

DO YOU KNOW . . . which player likes fruit in his/her water?

TRUTH Who is the most important person in the world to you?

DARE You are a flight attendant. Demonstrate some of the safety features of your aircraft.

DO YOU KNOW . . . what city/town the player to your right was born in?

43

TRUTH Describe the last time you were truly frightened.

DARE Stick your head under the faucet.

DO YOU KNOW . . . which player does his/her chores on time?

44

TRUTH What three words would you teach a parrot, if you had one?

DARE Walk in a crabwalk across the room while balancing something on your stomach.

DO YOU KNOW . . . which player orders buttered popcorn at the movies?

TRUTH or DARE

TRUTH   If you were a cat, who would you like your owner to be?

DARE   Pull up your nose and oink like a hungry pig.

DO YOU KNOW . . . what each player prefers: hot dog, hamburger or tofu?

TRUTH   What's the best song you could wake up to?

DARE   Call a friend and ask if you can borrow 60 cents.

DO YOU KNOW . . . which player has the largest CD collection?

47

TRUTH What would be the best thing about being the opposite gender?

DARE You've just come across the player to your left's diary. Pretend to read a juicy passage out loud to the group.

DO YOU KNOW ... the name(s) of the player to your right's sibling(s)?

48

TRUTH Describe a time you felt like a real dork.

DARE Put your finger in your ear, then pull it out and lick it.

DO YOU KNOW ... how to spell each player's last name?

TRUTH OR DARE

49 **TRUTH** What was your mom's pet name for you when you were little?

DARE Phone a friend and ask for advice about whether or not you should buy a new pair of socks.

DO YOU KNOW ... which player has cheated when playing hide-and-seek?

 50 **TRUTH** Have you ever picked wax out of your ear in a public place?

DARE Pick a nearby object and "show-and-tell" it to the group.

DO YOU KNOW ... which player sometimes forgets to wash his/her hands after going to the bathroom?

51 **TRUTH** How often do you wash your hair?

DARE Write a three-line poem called "An Ode to Nose Picking," then do a dramatic reading of it.

DO YOU KNOW ... which player can count to 10 in a foreign language?

52 **TRUTH** Which player would you say was the cutest baby?

DARE You're a robot. Dance and sing at least one chorus of "Mr. Roboto."

DO YOU KNOW ... which player talks in his/her sleep?

TRUTH OR DARE

53 **TRUTH** How much money do you have in your piggy bank?

DARE Rub noses with the player of your choice.

DO YOU KNOW . . . which player blushes easily?

54 **TRUTH** If you were stuck in an elevator, which classmate would you want to rescue you?

DARE Keep your eyes closed for an entire round.

DO YOU KNOW . . . which player can count to 10 in Spanish?

55 **TRUTH** Which player would you hate to have as a parent?

DARE Recite the theme song to the cartoon chosen by the player across from you.

DO YOU KNOW ... which player would rather live with mice than harm them?

56 **TRUTH** What's your favorite thing about yourself?

DARE Pick the player in the group you think would "go easiest" on you and do whatever s/he dares you to do.

DO YOU KNOW ... the player to your right's favorite brand of soda?

TRUTH OR DARE

57

TRUTH While setting the table, you drop your bratty brother's biscuit on the floor. Do you get him a new one or give it to him anyway?

DARE Compliment the player to your left using only words that begin with the letter "m."

DO YOU KNOW ... which player has had stitches?

58

TRUTH Name the movie you would star in if you could have the lead in any movie ever made.

DARE Pretend to milk a cow.

DO YOU KNOW ... which player has the best hair?

59

TRUTH Who would you call for advice if you had questions about boys/girls?

DARE Pretend to slow dance with your dream girl/boy.

DO YOU KNOW . . . which players believe in ghosts?

60

TRUTH If you had to give up one of the five senses (sight, hearing, touch, smell, taste), which one would it be?

DARE Pretend you're in the shower and pantomime what you'd be doing. Keep it clean!

DO YOU KNOW . . . which player has been in a play or musical?

TRUTH OR DARE

35

61 TRUTH Your new boy/girlfriend bakes you a birthday cake that tastes like glue. What do you do?

DARE Call a friend and tell them how excited you are about this week's ketchup sale at the grocery store.

DO YOU KNOW . . . which player has allergies?

62 TRUTH Have you ever passed gas—and blamed it on someone else?

DARE Rub your stomach and pat your head at the same time.

DO YOU KNOW . . . which players have been to Europe?

63

TRUTH What sport would you like to play professionally?

DARE Speak the chorus to a well-known love song into the ear of the player on your left. Don't sing!

DO YOU KNOW . . . which player has had the most school detentions?

64

TRUTH Ever opened someone else's e-mail and read it without telling him/her? If yes, give details.

DARE Give the player to your left an Eskimo kiss (nose to nose).

DO YOU KNOW . . . which player likes peas?

TRUTH OR DARE

 TRUTH Which movie star would you most like to share a scene with?

DARE Sing "Rain, Rain Go Away" and let the player to your left flick water at you.

DO YOU KNOW... which player has been snowboarding?

 TRUTH What player's phone would you most like to tap?

DARE Wear your shoes on your hands until your next turn.

DO YOU KNOW... which player is the youngest?

TRUTH What's the worst thing a friend has ever done to you?

DARE You're a butterfly about to hatch from your cocoon. Show us the metamorphosis.

DO YOU KNOW . . . what players have seen a play on Broadway?

TRUTH If you could give your parents any one gift in the world, what would it be?

DARE Say "and I've got gas" after everything you say for the next five minutes.

DO YOU KNOW . . . which player has eaten a bug?

TRUTH OR DARE

39

69

TRUTH Which player is most likely to sneak a peek at his/her birthday gift?

DARE Let the player to your left draw a tattoo that says "I [heart] Mom" on your forearm.

DO YOU KNOW . . . which players can breakdance?

70

TRUTH Describe the best family vacation you've ever had.

DARE Quack and waddle like a duck.

DO YOU KNOW . . . which player tends to burn his/her toast?

71 **TRUTH** Tell the player to your left something that bugs you about him/her.

DARE Pull out a piece of hair from your head and floss your teeth with it. (If your hair is too short, use another player's.)

DO YOU KNOW ... which player knows what fruit helps prevent sailors from getting scurvy?

72 **TRUTH** How old were you when you gave up your security blanket?

DARE Applaud everything that the player to your right says for the next two rounds.

DO YOU KNOW ... which player interrupts people the most?

TRUTH OR DARE

41

73 **TRUTH** When was the last time you cut in line?

DARE Lie down on your stomach and pull yourself across the room using only your elbows.

DO YOU KNOW ... which player was a Girl/Boy Scout?

 74 **TRUTH** Which player is most likely to talk his/her way out of trouble?

DARE Play an imaginary harp.

DO YOU KNOW ... which player has peed his/her pants in the last two years?

TRUTH What's the last good deed someone's done for you?

DARE You're a Golden Retriever. Using your mouth, fetch something nearby and drop it in the lap of the player to your right.

DO YOU KNOW ... which player flossed his/her teeth last night?

TRUTH What is your least favorite fashion trend?

DARE You're Tweety Bird. Tell the other players why you'd make a great twuck dwiver.

DO YOU KNOW ... the first name of the player to your right's mom?

TRUTH OR DARE

TRUTH Name the grossest thing you've ever eaten.

DARE Pretend that you're blowing up a really, really large balloon.

DO YOU KNOW ... which player likes meatloaf?

TRUTH Do you think you have a guardian angel? If so, when is the last time you think it was watching over you?

DARE Touch your ears with your feet any way you can.

DO YOU KNOW ... which player collects things and what s/he collects?

TRUTH If you needed a transplant and could clone anyone's heart, whose heart would it be?

DARE Act like an angry mime until your next turn.

DO YOU KNOW... which player can name three characters on *SpongeBob SquarePants*?

TRUTH Describe one time that you tortured an insect. (☹)

DARE Give your best interpretation of a chick hatching from its egg.

DO YOU KNOW... which player likes maraschino cherries?

TRUTH OR DARE

81

TRUTH If you could have anyone's wardrobe, whose would it be?

DARE Pretend you're so dizzy that you can barely stand up straight.

DO YOU KNOW ... which player has never changed a baby's diaper?

82

TRUTH If you could have season tickets for any sports team, which team would it be?

DARE You're Bart Simpson. Bend over and sing "A Spoonful of Sugar Helps the Medicine Go Down."

DO YOU KNOW ... which player was born closest to the ocean?

TRUTH When's the last time you made your parents really mad?

DARE Pretend you're a cow with the deepest voice in the pasture and moo "Old MacDonald."

DO YOU KNOW ... what the player to your left considers his/her lucky number?

TRUTH If you had triplet daughters today, what would you name them?

DARE It's St. Patrick's Day and you forgot to wear green. Let each player show you the consequences.

DO YOU KNOW ... which player has a food allergy?

TRUTH OR DARE

85 **TRUTH** Have you ever had the same dream twice? What was it about?

DARE Get down on all fours, wag your behind and sing "How Much is that Doggy in the Window?"

DO YOU KNOW . . . which players are *not* wearing socks? No peeking!

86 **TRUTH** Name the one thing that always makes you smile.

DARE Sing the "Beans, Beans the Magical Fruit" song. Wrap it up with a big fake toot!

DO YOU KNOW . . . what the player to your left had for breakfast this morning?

87

TRUTH Name one thing you've done to bug your brother or sister.

DARE Call a relative on the phone and try to sell him/her a nose-hair clipper.

DO YOU KNOW ... which player looks most like his/her mom?

88

TRUTH If you could have one type of snack always stocked in your kitchen cupboard, what would it be?

DARE You're Chicken Little. Scurry nervously around the room repeating, "the sky is falling" 10 times.

DO YOU KNOW ... which players prefer chocolate to vanilla?

TRUTH OR DARE

49

89 **TRUTH** Which player is most likely from outer space?

DARE Blow your best spit bubble.

DO YOU KNOW ... which player ate pizza most recently?

90 **TRUTH** If you could talk to any type of animal, which would it be?

DARE Give a sales pitch to the group for a new product called the "Hankyshmelt."

DO YOU KNOW ... which player has played "Light as a Feather, Stiff as a Board"?

91 **TRUTH** Would you rather be Spiderman® or Peter Parker?

DARE Imitate Porky Pig s-s-singing "I Got You, Babe."

DO YOU KNOW . . . which player has the most change in his/her
pockets right now?

92 **TRUTH** Grandma gives you an ugly sweater. What do you do: wear it,
toss it or give it away?

DARE Act like a monkey.

DO YOU KNOW . . . which player still sleeps with a
stuffed animal?

TRUTH Which player would you peg as a schoolyard bully?

DARE There's a new dance craze called the "Tiger Woods Swing" sweeping the nation. Show us how it goes.

DO YOU KNOW . . . which player will take clothing out of the dirty clothes hamper to wear?

 TRUTH If you could hypnotize someone for one day, who would it be and what would you have him/her do?

DARE Hold hands with the player on your right until your next turn.

DO YOU KNOW . . . which player can name at least one local newscaster?

95

TRUTH   You are introduced to the president of the United States. What one thing do you say to him?

DARE   Let the player on your right draw a happy face on your thumb.

DO YOU KNOW . . . who didn't shower today?

96

TRUTH   Describe the worst family vacation you've ever been on.

DARE   Pretend you are a cheerleader and do a cheer for the others.

DO YOU KNOW . . . which player gets mostly As in school?

TRUTH OR DARE

97

TRUTH The lottery has reached $80 million. Do you buy a ticket?

DARE Take off another player's sock with your teeth.

DO YOU KNOW ... which player goes to church regularly?

98

TRUTH Which player is most likely to peek out from under the blindfold when playing Blind Man's Bluff?

DARE Using only one word, describe the player to your right.

DO YOU KNOW ... which player has never been skiing?

99 TRUTH Which player is most likely to share his/her lunch with you?

DARE Stand on your head for one minute.

DO YOU KNOW ... which player still watches cartoons?

100 TRUTH You are on the Titanic as it's sinking. There's one life vest left for you and your closest friend. What do you do?

DARE Pretend you're Cookie Monster and eat some cookies.

DO YOU KNOW ... what kind of lunchbox the player to your right carries?

TRUTH OR DARE

101 **TRUTH** What's the best gift you've ever given?

DARE Read the palm of the player to your right and predict his/her future.

DO YOU KNOW . . . the player to your left's middle name?

102 **TRUTH** Which player's pet do you like the least?

DARE Demonstrate the first five ballet positions. If you don't know them, make them up!

DO YOU KNOW . . . the middle name of the player to your left?

103 TRUTH You're home alone and run out of toilet paper. What do you do?

DARE Do 20 pushups. Have the other players count down.

DO YOU KNOW . . . the last TV show seen by the person on your left?

104 TRUTH Which player would be least likely to survive, if stranded on a deserted island?

DARE Let the player to your left use your lap as a footrest until your next turn.

DO YOU KNOW . . . which player has the biggest feet?

TRUTH OR DARE

105 TRUTH A car in the parking lot has its lights on. What do you do?

DARE Draw a fake moustache on yourself.

DO YOU KNOW ... the phone number of the player to your right by heart?

106 TRUTH Describe what you wore in your first-grade school picture.

DARE Drink three eight-ounce glasses of water before your next turn.

DO YOU KNOW ... at least one thing that is under the player to your left's bed?

107 TRUTH If you could talk to one person, dead or alive, who would it be?

DARE Try to do the yoga pose called "lotus." If you don't know it, make it up.

DO YOU KNOW ... who keeps a diary?

108 TRUTH If you could move to one place for the rest of your life, where would it be?

DARE Stick your tongue out and wink at the same time.

DO YOU KNOW ... what the player to your left's favorite board game is?

TRUTH OR DARE

109 **TRUTH** Tell the group the name of your imaginary friend when you were a child.

DARE Get down on your knees and sing "You are my Sunshine" to the player on your left.

DO YOU KNOW . . . what the player to your right's dream car is?

110 **TRUTH** You're a star. What's your stage name?

DARE Pick your nose in front of the other players.

DO YOU KNOW . . . what color house or apartment building the player to your right lives in?

111

TRUTH Which player would be the best business partner and why?

DARE Call a friend and pretend that s/he is the one who called you.

DO YOU KNOW ... which players are the youngest children in their families?

112

TRUTH If you were stuck on a deserted island with only one CD to listen to, which one would it be?

DARE You're in the library. Whisper till your next turn.

DO YOU KNOW ... what was the first concert the player to your left attended?

TRUTH OR DARE

113 TRUTH Which player is most likely to walk into a sliding glass door?

DARE You are running for treasurer of your class. Give a speech and see how many votes you can win.

DO YOU KNOW ... which player prefers bran flakes to frosted flakes for breakfast?

114 TRUTH If your house was on fire and you could grab only one thing, what would it be?

DARE Give everyone in the group a nickname that rhymes with his/her real name.

DO YOU KNOW ... what wish the player to your right would make if today were his/her birthday?

115

TRUTH   Confess a white lie that you've told to someone in the group.

DARE   The player to your right is a cop and has just pulled you over for speeding. Talk your way out of the ticket.

DO YOU KNOW ... which player still takes bubble baths?

116

TRUTH   Name the player you could take down most easily in a wrestling match.

DARE   You're running for 6th-grade president. Give us your speech.

DO YOU KNOW ... which player has the most dental fillings?

TRUTH OR DARE

117 **TRUTH**   Name a song you're embarrassed to admit you like.

DARE   Belch as much of the alphabet as you can.

DO YOU KNOW ... which player snores?

118 **TRUTH**   Who have you flirted with most recently?

DARE   Pretend that you've just put a large spoonful of peanut butter in your mouth and tell us about your day.

DO YOU KNOW ... which player has an "outie" bellybutton?

119

TRUTH   Do you always remember to say please and thank you?

DARE   Channel the spirit of Elvis Presley and let him speak through you, baby.

DO YOU KNOW ... which player is camera shy?

120

TRUTH   Which player do you think would plan the best birthday party?

DARE   Examine the bottom of the player to your left's shoe.

DO YOU KNOW ... which player can say hello in French?

TRUTH OR DARE

65

121 **TRUTH** Which player most needs his/her mouth washed out with soap?

DARE Pretend you're a cat and give yourself a "bath."

DO YOU KNOW . . . which player has an iPod®?

122 **TRUTH** What word is most embarrassing for you to say?

DARE Sit on the ground and try to put one leg behind your head.

DO YOU KNOW . . . which player has rescued an injured animal?

123

TRUTH   What is the biggest lie you've ever told?

DARE   Let the player to your left make up a dare for you.

DO YOU KNOW . . . which player plays soccer?

124

TRUTH   Describe a time that you laughed when you shouldn't have.

DARE   Pick another player to stand behind you and let yourself fall back into his/her arms.

DO YOU KNOW . . . which player has written to a pen pal?

TRUTH OR DARE

67

125 **TRUTH** What's the most fun you've had at a slumber party?

DARE You're a mime in a box. Show us how you get out.

DO YOU KNOW ... which player talks to him/herself when alone?

126 **TRUTH** When is the last time you felt left out?

DARE Balance a spoon on your nose for at least three seconds.

DO YOU KNOW ... which player can name all seven of Snow White's dwarfs?

TRUTH How much money would it take to get you to run around the block in your underwear?

DARE Don't use your thumbs for the next three minutes.

DO YOU KNOW ... the names of the pet(s) belonging to the person on your right?

TRUTH You notice a dog owner not clean up after his dog. What do you do?

DARE You've gotta go and someone's in the bathroom. Let us see you hold it untill your next turn.

DO YOU KNOW ... which player has the most pennies in his/her pocket?

129 **TRUTH** A person that you don't like offers to help you do a tough homework assignment. Do you let them help you?

DARE Your teeth just fell out! Talk without them untill your next turn.

DO YOU KNOW . . . which player is a secret slob—and will admit it?

130 **TRUTH** Name one thing that makes you happy.

DARE With your head back, arms out and eyes closed, walk as if you're on a tightrope.

DO YOU KNOW . . . which player can say hello in Spanish?

131 **TRUTH** What's your best quality?

DARE Do your most annoying laugh until someone in the group tells you to stop.

DO YOU KNOW ... which player has a birthmark?

 132 **TRUTH** What's the first thing you thought of when you woke up this morning?

DARE Pretend to walk backwards on a balance beam.

DO YOU KNOW ... what the ethnic background is of the player to your left?

TRUTH OR DARE

133

TRUTH If you're in a big hurry and you see that there's an easy way to cut in line, do you do it?

DARE Spin in a circle 10 times.

DO YOU KNOW ... which player's dad has a moustache?

134

TRUTH What movie do you quote most often? Prove it.

DARE Make three sounds that are usually related to being in the bathroom.

DO YOU KNOW ... which player had/has a tree house?

135   **TRUTH**   Who do you most admire? Why?

          DARE   Ask your neighbor if you can borrow a pair of socks.

          DO YOU KNOW . . . which player writes in block print?

136   **TRUTH**   Which *Harry Potter* character do you identify with most, and why?

          DARE   Make art out of something in the trash and try to sell it to the player to your left.

          DO YOU KNOW . . . which player likes black licorice?

TRUTH OR DARE

137 **TRUTH** If you had to share your Chapstick® with a classmate, who would it be?

DARE Lick another player's hand.

DO YOU KNOW . . . which players can crack their knuckles?

 138 **TRUTH** Name three things that make you a good friend.

DARE Phone a friend and wish him/her "Happy Bellybutton Appreciation Day."

DO YOU KNOW . . . how many pets the player to your left has?

139

TRUTH   Describe the worst hairstyle you've ever had.

DARE   Pull one hair out of your head for each person playing, excluding yourself.

DO YOU KNOW ... what color underwear the player to your right is wearing?

140

TRUTH   If you had to eat the same thing for a whole week, what would it be?

DARE   Have a staring contest with the player to your right. Go the longest without blinking and win!

DO YOU KNOW ... which player can play a musical instrument?

TRUTH OR DARE

141 TRUTH What's the most embarrassing thing you've ever said in class?

DARE Lead the group in a meditation on the beauty of "invisible" tape.

DO YOU KNOW ... which player prefers veggies over meat?

142 TRUTH What do you want to be when you grow up?

DARE How low can you go? Show the other players your lowest limbo.

DO YOU KNOW ... which player has the biggest hands?

143

TRUTH Have you ever pretended to be someone else?

DARE Put an ice cube on your head and keep it there until it melts.

DO YOU KNOW . . . which player took swimming lessons?

144

TRUTH Has anyone ever walked in on you in the bathroom?

DARE Open up, say "ahh!" and let everyone get a good look at your dental work.

DO YOU KNOW . . . which player is least likely to forgive you after a fight?

TRUTH OR DARE

TRUTH Describe the time your mother or father embarrassed you most.

DARE Stand up and recite the Pledge of Allegiance. Come on, you should know this!

DO YOU KNOW . . . the player to your left's favorite dessert?

TRUTH Describe a time you've felt jealous when something good happened to one of your friends.

DARE Allow each player to pinch your cheeks and say, "Look how much you've grown!"

DO YOU KNOW . . . which player drinks straight from the milk carton?

147 **TRUTH** What is the one thing you'd change about your house, if you could?

DARE Have the player to your right pinch you on the arm.

DO YOU KNOW ... which player most recently rode a horse?

148 **TRUTH** Name the one book you would like to have with you if you were stranded on a deserted island.

DARE You've been told to walk the plank. Now beg and plead your way out of it, you scurvy pirate.

DO YOU KNOW ... which player has mowed lawns or sold lemonade for money?

TRUTH OR DARE

149 TRUTH If you could be any animal in your next life, what animal would it be?

DARE Try to convince the player to your left to buy your shirt for more than it's worth. Sell it!

DO YOU KNOW . . . which player believes that there is life on other planets?

150 TRUTH Name the one superpower you'd like to have.

DARE Use whistling as your only form of communication until your next turn.

DO YOU KNOW . . . which player has played dodgeball in the last two years?

151 **TRUTH** What do you think is the most difficult thing about being a kid today?

DARE Sing a well-known pop/rock song as if it were a solemn church hymn.

DO YOU KNOW ... which player has been on a roller coaster most recently?

152 **TRUTH** Who would you call if you were kidnapped and allowed only ONE phone call?

DARE Phone a friend and ask if you can borrow an ice cube.

DO YOU KNOW ... which player has bought something online within the last three months?

TRUTH OR DARE

81

153 **TRUTH**   Ever read someone else's diary? Share the details.

DARE   Pretend you're the Queen of England and knight the player to your left.

DO YOU KNOW . . . which player would make the best cheerleader?

154 **TRUTH**   If you could change the number of siblings you have, what would you change it to?

DARE   Do your best boy band dance.

DO YOU KNOW . . . what year the player to your left started kindergarten?

155

TRUTH If you could be invisible for one day, where would you go and what would you do?

DARE Let the player to your left mess up your hair.

DO YOU KNOW ... which player is the biggest packrat?

156

TRUTH What trait would you like to pass on to your kids?

DARE You're a baby dinosaur about to hatch. Show us the miracle of life and hatch from the egg.

DO YOU KNOW ... which player has broken a bone?

TRUTH OR DARE

83

157 **TRUTH** If you could trade houses with someone you know, who would it be?

DARE You're a snake about to molt. Slither across the room and shed your skin.

DO YOU KNOW . . . which player has tried escargot?

 158 **TRUTH** Would you lick the seat of a public toilet for a thousand dollars?

DARE Say, "she sells seashells by the sea shore" five times.

DO YOU KNOW . . . which player knows what a turkey baster is for?

159

TRUTH Describe a dream you had about another player, but never shared.

DARE Say, "and I just let one fly" after everything you say for the next three minutes.

DO YOU KNOW . . . who's a Mac lover and who's a PC lover?

160

TRUTH If the player to your right were a car, what make or model would s/he be? Why?

DARE Using your body as an instrument, play "Jingle Bells."

DO YOU KNOW . . . which players have been to the opera?

TRUTH OR DARE

85

161 **TRUTH** What physical characteristic about yourself reminds you of one of your parents?

DARE Do the worm across the room.

DO YOU KNOW ... which player prefers plain M&Ms® to peanut?

162 **TRUTH** If you could go back in time and witness one event from your family's history, what would it be?

DARE Stop, drop and roll across the room.

DO YOU KNOW ... which player doesn't like to play video games?

163

TRUTH Name the one household chore that you wish you never had to do again.

DARE Cross the length of the room as fast as you can without using your feet.

DO YOU KNOW ... which players say "God bless you" after someone sneezes?

164

TRUTH What breed would you be if you were reincarnated as a dog?

DARE Give another player a piggyback ride across the room.

DO YOU KNOW ... which player would rather hit the beach than the slopes?

TRUTH OR DARE

165

TRUTH If you could name only one song as the best song of all time, which would it be?

DARE You're a horse. Take the player to your left for a ride around the room.

DO YOU KNOW ... which player has cut his/her own hair?

166

TRUTH If a joke is told and everyone but you seems to "get it," do you pretend that you get it too, or ask the person who told it to explain?

DARE You're a fly. Buzz around the room and annoy people.

DO YOU KNOW ... which player can name at least one Judy Blume book?

167 **TRUTH** Do you look inside the tissue after you blow your nose?

DARE Bark and beg like a dog.

DO YOU KNOW ... which player knows who wrote *Oh, The Places You'll Go!*?

168 **TRUTH** Have you ever eaten food out of the garbage?

DARE Lie on your back and pedal your feet in the air for 30 seconds. (Your bottom should *not* touch the ground.)

DO YOU KNOW ... which player has been to Yosemite?

TRUTH OR DARE

169

TRUTH Do you think you'll make a good parent? Why?

DARE Pretend that you're in bed having a really, really funny dream.

DO YOU KNOW . . . which player likes to ride a skateboard?

170

TRUTH A person in front of you tosses a Styrofoam® cup on the ground. What do you do?

DARE Pretend you are a pirate and start every sentence with "Aye, matey" until your next turn.

DO YOU KNOW . . . the color of the other players' eyes?
(No looking!)

171 **TRUTH** Have you ever picked (your nose) and flicked?

DARE Pretend that you're being struck by lightning at this very moment!

DO YOU KNOW . . . which player can say the alphabet backwards without making a mistake?

172 **TRUTH** Have you ever sniffed your socks to see if they were clean?

DARE Using your whole body (not just your arms), shape yourself into the letter "u."

DO YOU KNOW . . . which player can do the best sick voice?

TRUTH or DARE

173 **TRUTH** Tell the story behind one of your scars.

DARE Do the chicken dance. Don't know it? Do it anyway.

DO YOU KNOW . . . which players are wearing shoes that lace? No peeking!

174 **TRUTH** Name one thing your parents are proud of you for.

DARE You've just been cast in a "Joy of Prune Juice" commercial. Act it out for us.

DO YOU KNOW . . . which player can name four *Peanuts* characters?

175 **TRUTH** If you could eliminate one form of weather, what would it be?

DARE Lick your elbow.

DO YOU KNOW . . . which player has taken tap dancing?

176 **TRUTH** Your dad accidentally gives you an extra $10 in allowance. Do you tell him?

DARE Using a mirror, take a pen and write the player to your right's name on your forehead.

DO YOU KNOW . . . which player has read *Charlotte's Web?*

TRUTH OR DARE

93

177

TRUTH Have you ever tattletaled on someone? Who? Why?

DARE With all of your heart, audition for the next big teeny-bopper band.

DO YOU KNOW . . . which player could stop a runaway camel?

178

TRUTH Describe your favorite memory.

DARE As fast as you can, talk nonstop about whatever comes into your head for one full minute. No stopping!

DO YOU KNOW . . . which player always asks, "Do I have food in my teeth?"

179

TRUTH   Name an actor or musician that you had (or still have!) a huge crush on.

DARE   Teach the other players how to country line dance, even if you have to make it up.

DO YOU KNOW . . . which player sleeps on his/her stomach?

180

TRUTH   What was your favorite book when you were younger?

DARE   Make the silliest face you can and accompany it with sound effects.

DO YOU KNOW . . . what the player to your left's favorite TV show is?

TRUTH OR DARE

ABOUT THE AUTHOR

BOB MOOG, co-founder of University Games and publisher of Spinner Books™ and Armchair Puzzlers™, has been creating games, brainteasers, word puzzles and the like since childhood. He tormented his four younger siblings with quizzes, conundrums and fun physical and mental challenges during the 1960s. Now, he introduces the Made You Laugh for Kids™ series, hoping it will amuse you as much as his early "work" amused his family 40 years ago.

Moog is the author of several other puzzle, game and children's books, including *Gummy Bear Goes to Camp, 20 Questions*®, *30 Second Mysteries*™ and *Secret Identities*. He hasn't peed his pants in a long time.